Dreaming Alone and with Others

Gerald Yelle

FUTURECYCLE PRESS
www.futurecycle.org

Cover design and photo by Gerald Yelle; author photo by Geneva Yelle; interior design by Diane Kistner; Minion Pro text and Jost titling

Library of Congress Control Number: 2022944645

Published by FutureCycle Press
Athens, Georgia, USA

ISBN 978-1-952593-37-6

For Jenny

Contents

I. Message Boards

II. Playbills

III. Forgeries

I. Message Boards

It Starts

It’s in the whistling of the kettle:
a wordless whisper I feel
more than hear, that has me
steel myself while bending.
I straighten up and soften,
walk through solids hollow
and cross my heart and three
swift rivers. I shield my
eyes in sugar towns where
neighbors drill through neighbors’
walls and work my way
to comfort zones in olive
grove casinos. I play the game
of *Silence Is Golden* in
open-carry colonies and bury
treasure in oblong boxes
labeled “silence = death.”
I read the signs while bending.
I soften up and straighten.
I harden when I’m bent
and bending gets me through.

The Babe the Clock the Deer

The town hall's clock had been broken
so long
I set my watch by the fall of a toddler.
I waited at the bus stop
as she held her breath till her face
turned orange
—giving rise to thoughts
of the spring at its source shedding tears.

And the scrape on her knee and the cut
on her cheek made her hold her clocked-up
breath till her face turned purple

till a nod, a wink, a crumb on the cob
on the curb, a pigeon hooked
on kerosene fumes, a mother refusing
to look or take pity

the child clocking out with fisted candor
the mother saying
"What if Grandma sees you like this?"
with the dazed gaze of a
car-struck fawn bleeding from the ticker.

Silver Queen Corn

Sandalwood tracks into lavender.
Varnish backs into cane.
It's on the way to my father's with his
bath off the kitchen like his mother's
with its smell like rotting soil
—though his breath was a kid's once,
his lanolin chin rough on my cheek
on certain unshaved days.
You should've seen him bagging groceries
while a TB stranglehold polished
off his father. He forged
frugal habits, forwent wild oats
so he could raise a family.
I know every living thing has this love
that drives the world. In time all
Suffrageola would console him
when his mother died.
A drink with the uncles: their sturdy
thighs and survivalist cunning.
A drink to the debt that hovers
like Monadnock above his
fruited plain. And though he's no
drinker, a toast to tongues cleaving
to palates. Bell claps at auction,
the acre unproductive.
A parachute's slow descent in rain.

Large Building in Which to Lay Aside Your Shame

Breaking into fleeting blear-eyed argument,
love in the auspices of rain.
At one extreme a pantheist needing
nothing more than looking once and moving on.
Barhop from door to door in the cold
Lord knows, you start getting furtive.
Needing the rainbow's hallway.
Needing meeting need to meet my match.
Which happens, and afterwards
violence. And silence.
Imaginary violence, oneself imaginary
in the minds of a few individuals.
Hardly able to get up in the morning without one's angel.

And what if I'm infantile,
and cheap? Intent on using
everything, rough rush, lush lust,
never known to eschew a low motive,
I volunteer Angel Cabrera,
whose unobtrusive entrance
a year ago in June sparked an opening in Soho.
A wingspan when fully extended
like the roofline of an expandable cape.
Aunt in bestial dreams I would have
set my sights on if I had seen.
She whispered in my ear
she had a battleship
the size of Hitler's Nautilus
and that was all it took to haul me in.

Falling out was trading wings for gender
and claiming to be neither.
"Storm the gates," they'd say.
"Take me either way and let me know."
The first hour passed with little progress.
I guess I've been lucky. I must have been blessed.
A series of wide, white days
for when I stopped floating like a leaf
mid-air, cornered leghorns
kicking sawdust on the bar-barn floor.

Kisses stood out cold on fretful brows.
“It’s what men do with mentors,”
he’d say. He’d say he
still has the flex I found so
enchanting in his female Avatar.
In Scout camp, a tent mate undressing
I forced to talk about his sister.
I could hide my excitement from anyone
but Angel Cabrera.
In three weeks the clocks turn.
Angular limbs gaining momentum.
A month and he’ll be gone.
Leprechaun gone to burn in Tennessee.
Gone his courage to the Crossville knights
better suited to his style
than in Wheeling, with its river.

Big Blind Little Blind

Other girls wore peasant shirts and faded jeans.
Her long-sleeved, starched white button-downs
and pleated skirts set her apart. As did her
colorless cheek—rendered even paler in her
dark hair's frame, and silence. Most of us knew
little about her—we lived on different streets
and sat in different classes. And when she
stepped off the bus and fell to the sidewalk
in one more grand mal we gave her space:
"It's a seizure, it'll pass." Some of us wondered
about her parents. Maybe she'd been epileptic
since early childhood and they trusted
strangers to help if she fell in the street.
But what about them legs? Most turned away
when her skirt rode up to show a mile
of thigh. We were that mature—most of us.
But who wouldn't want to kiss a thigh
grab a hank of hair, see if a slap wouldn't
bring her round? Nineteen out of twenty
she'd be off the bus walking with her head
held high. Did it feel like a sneeze
coming on? Did she dream more lucky days
than she could ever hope to count while
writhing in her slow-motion moan and jerk?

This Is My Letter to the World

There's an inner violence I can't
disguise—an anger that jumps
and grabs—that hides behind everyday
objects and erupts when the comfort
level drops below the waterline.
Sometimes you're busy and I have
something to say and I know you
don't want that kind of influence
and I don't want you to have it—but
there you are, you mean the world.
And neither of us can do what we
don't already. It's just that life is full
of noise and additional require-
ments. I don't want to bring it up
because neither of us needs reminding
but we have to keep the phones
charged and throw away the clocks.
And here comes my sister with
her Charles DeGaulle avidity that
never fails to get her in trouble.
I don't say it's something I have to
help with but I have to tell myself
she doesn't so much take me for
granted as fail to see that we might
have problems of our own. I should
be glad our problems are not the
same as hers—they're minute by
comparison. Frankly I'm ashamed
at how small they are. But forget that.
It's not what I wanted to say.

Rust

Puddles and shiners line
the street where you
trade your car for kisses
in the morning and sob
in the evening when your
lover won't stay in bed:
a low moan the light is
slow to cover. If she hears
she'll leave and nothing
can stop her from hearing:
Distant traffic. Crows
and doves. A wood thrush
insecurity. A 60-cycle
hum, some tinnitus from
standing close to a megaphone.
The sound of ink and
breathing: Guitars squeak
and cut some difficult
maneuvers. They ship
and handle physical bodies
while other physical
bodies play the melody.

Mark of the Squealer

He stomped up the stairs three at a time
banged on the door and hollered
all of it echoing up and down and all
around the stairwell: "Marlene, get your
ass out here. Open the goddamned
door. Right now." We never knew if she
was there. Didn't stay awake
long enough to know what happened
or if she was cheating. No memory
of her moving either—she was simply
replaced by a woman who had
a voice like a carpet knife. Her man
would come in, four in the morning.
She'd demand to know where he'd been.
He'd say, "There's the phone. I'm sure
your so-called friends can tell you."
She'd warn her kid to stay away from
construction sites. She found him after
one nerve-wracking search
up to his neck in dirt, a scar running
from his ear to the corner of his mouth.

What Though the Haze Burn

Eve doesn't seem to mind
if her husband looks for work
and I suppose I don't care.
I mean it's not as if he can
muscle in on us. He has
scant skills and nil will.
He's too busy wondering
who ate his egg to worry about
who might be doing his wife.
He's like an obstruction
in the midst of our small
intestinal summer. Music
fraught with fragrance
rises from the warehouse
and basks in the aisles of
shipping and deceiving as if
housewares were cold and riffs
the sole source of steam.

After Scuttling the Shuttle

The parallels were there: The wife
like the brother—hadn't you slept with
both at different stages? The airport
and the golf course: both at different
points crowded in displays of hurried
affection. Husbands kissing wives.
Actors making bones about fences
making good neighbors: a restaurant
in place of a rug shop. And your
father, I'm sorry to hear he's unwell.
None of your extras could peel a di-
lemma with anywhere near the scorn
he so carelessly tossed in his wake.
He'd ache with the first casual revel
he'd smell on the beach: You won't
find his like in any two-dimensional
hotspot. You check it out, check
the mirror, contrive a smile, a candle
in the window, a toy under the bed.

Umbria for Cambridge

A magic lamp with phthalo-blue
bulb supposed to cure the Bilirubin
but all it did was turn him orange.
He'd doze, nurse, occasionally cry.
His mother hadn't eaten. His father
hadn't slept and would've bought
apples but for the flies that plagued
the stalls. The mother would've
nibbled around the specks. She was
that hungry. The father wandered
hospital streets unable to see where
the light was inadequate. It had been
a long vigil. The weather turned
sultry. Masonry crumbled, rolled
from plastic sheets hung like umber
tiles in marble skies. Inpatients
padded by: the only other mammals
on the grounds, their gazes downcast,
their smiles unhinged by halftrack
rumblings. Unsettling but there'd soon
come a night when the whole world
slept and it felt as a feeling feels
that masks for a time our collective
dread as if we could drift for decades
of days without coming to grief.

Meeting

We finished reviewing the first report to everyone's satisfaction. I excused myself to retrieve copies of the second report from my car. At no time did I criticize myself, either mentally or verbally, for not having had it with me when the meeting started. I considered it par for the course given the stress and chaos of the last few days. Besides, this meeting was scheduled last minute to fill in for some other activity that had to be canceled because the presenter was suddenly unavailable. I went out to the garage

but I never did make it to my car. Workmen were backing a tractor-trailer in —a maneuver consisting of movement by inches and steering by degrees. I waited to squeeze around the front of the cab. Then I saw an old flatbed I'd never noticed before rusting in a corner and couldn't resist the urge to pull out my wrench and take the nuts off a few bolts—for old time's sake. I have to say it felt good. It took a little longer than it should've but while I was doing it I reasoned that the report I needed might not actually be in the car. While I couldn't be absolutely certain, I had the vague suspicion

that a coworker who had been in the meeting earlier might be in possession of it. She was in the ninth month of a tricky pregnancy and had excused herself for a doctor's appointment, with the promise that she'd return well before we finished. I wasn't taking any chances, however. I left the garage just as they were closing up, ducked under the big doors, and made my way up to the birthing unit where I ran into a doctor I used to work with. I asked if she'd seen the coworker in question. She responded positively,

but cautioned that I was in a restricted area and couldn't stay. As I headed back down the stairs she and her colleagues called after me with questions concerning the coworker's pregnancy, asking if I knew why she hadn't told her parents which made me think we weren't talking about the same person. There was a pregnant sixteen-year-old in the neighborhood and I wondered if that's who they were referring to. When they asked if I could take a message to the baby's father, let him know he wasn't welcome in the ward, I knew right then, by the time I got there, the meeting would be over.

Perpetual Help Destroyed by Fire

In their respective books both Proust and Galeano tell of churches that burn
while parish priests are out to pasture.

Ours burned along with several buildings and trees while the priest stood by and wept. He left
and brought back saplings to plant around the stumps and ruins.

He left his shovel in the rain and covered his face in ashes.
He walked and pondered. He pondered and prayed. Knelt in frozen trenches, did pointless calisthenics,
dug up relics and raised funds by holding raffles.

Evening shadows of fruit bats on clay pots and glass jars on dusty shelves:
He hears their echoes and the echoes of his calling.
They fly by fixed approximations: closing in, never striking home.

Volleyball Bivalve

Tom and I took each other for granted, having shared
the same birthday, attended the same daycare
and sat in the same classes. We assumed
shared experience would shape similar attitudes.
By middle school it was clear it wouldn't.
He became athletic and made fun of my flubs.
But even he met his match when a man
came to school to teach life lessons by beating us
at volleyball. Tom sprained his back
diving after the first serve. The guy kept
winning no matter how many prodigies
we sent in. He'd toss the serve high and not even
look. We had no idea where it was going
until it came whizzing at our ankles.
I guess that must've been the lesson:
One man can take a whole school with the right
spin speed and angle. I might've played
in college but the team already had
a hundred guys and Em was always in my room.
Early in our second year we discovered
that none of the doors locked. We got out
and married without probing one another's secrets.
What could I learn that she didn't reveal
in the course of a few shared meals?
One day the tide took her toward sharp rocks
and two lifeguards swam to the rescue
though neither of us thought she was in danger.
It's hard to predict serenity. We try
not to take advantage of one another's weaknesses.
We might yet discover that we're twins.

Setting the Table for Ever

Kids on sitcoms fuss over dimes. The ones at work throw them.
You try not to think about it.

The ones at home—at least as long as their phones are charged
are fine. Cain cuts his salad with a knife

and watches the iceberg brown. Noodles slide from Abel's fork.
You see the bind God's in: Do for one

and the other cries foul. You're tired—like a ghost. Never alone
in or out of the frame. Snow drops like beaten rain

and radioactive ash on rugs. The furnace blows. The kitchen
disposes. Ants inhale dreams of solitude

while concrete under the carpet absorbs the scent of jasmine.
It penetrates the wall of windows

and makes lust like so much that's repetitive: a carpal tunnel
of one-hit wonders that shows how

a board can bend with the lightest step and still read the code
of a child's cough. Or hear it as visual speech.

Rinka Deeva

Rainy nights and dark days raised the specter
of Independence Day fireworks at noon
—though it wasn't so cloudy that you got a decent look.
At least I got to see Bottle Baby
—one of my myriad daughters—up for the show.

I assumed she was down the street around
the corner visiting her
grandmother with a bunch of her other sisters
while I got her old attic room ready.
When the old woman came to ask about her

I immediately assumed the worst.
I looked everywhere inside and out
all the streets and avenues
—including the witch's crib in case the kid was
there and she simply hadn't noticed.
It was like the neighborhood swallowed her whole.

Bottle Baby wasn't like other kids.
She once let this girl sit near
her husband and said it was okay
as long as she left his veins and arteries alone.
Somehow her going AWOL
reminded me of that.

My neighbor was reading a poster on a lamp post:
A concert with Jack Veronesi and friends.
I asked if he was going. He shrugged.
I asked about his holiday.
He said "Merry Christmas" without looking up.
I said, "It isn't Christmas.
I asked how your holiday was, meaning the Fourth."

He said Merry. I said "Mine too" and went up
breathing hard from the endless
runaround. The attic was coming along
despite my interrupted efforts. I went to fetch the tools
I used to take down Christmas
decorations and banged my head on a nail.

At the Airport

Giant touch-screens on the concourse
show more than departures
and ETA's. Pull-down tabs let viewers
scroll through television programs
by town. Oh look, Brockton has
Mary Hartman. Lanesboro: *Captain*
Kangaroo. I know there's porn
in Petersham—no discrete way to
check it though. Besides, it's an airport
which itself is fascinating: sprawling
vistas swirling traffic, self-driving
cars and planes that cut up so
close one behind the other—something
humans could never do. Someone
says that the government wastes too
much money helping people
pay for education when it should be
making this place even bigger
and brighter. I defend the program
albeit in a shaky voice. I say
"My mother argued a case before a federal
judge this very day having recently
passed the bar all because of
that excessive educational funding."
They ask my mother's age.
I say eighty. That part at least is true.

II. Playbills

Land of Little Sticks Again

Dawn's chirp unlocks the registry
so the sheep can feel like bison
and the sewer trunks act like brain-
stems, leaving the crows the traffic
to contend with. They do
comprehend the solid yellow line
but a corbie eating a fry is like
a man who doesn't know
to tame the grossness of his appetite
—he has to feel a crumbling
in the underpinning. He no longer
responds to switches. Some of them
swell the moly of a late summer sky:
a divestiture that beckons
to the tendril. A sadness in one casts
a shadow on another. A humming-
bird entered a shed by mistake
and lost its strength searching for
a breach in the screen.
It sips the dregs at the bottom of
a small plastic cup. Twa corbies
take care not to dream too loud,
not to slam and collide when they
pay the open house a second visit.
They make a sandwich and
hope the ghost mistakes them for
hummingbirds. They don't
give the names they used last time
when they overwound the clocks,
clogged the pipes, marred
the milk and spat in the quern.

Hey Herm, look at Snout: dressed like a wall!

Hay is for horses, Ly, and you'd be a hell of a Pyramus
with your curious cold heat. You do see how this
could be us. Was it yesterday our trip through the forest
put a crimp in Dad's plan? I don't know what would
be worse: a father's kiss of death or the convent Theseus
picked out for me. Then running in the night: if only
we hadn't got lost—and you hadn't hit on my BFF.
I ran into Demetrius when you ran after her. I didn't know
where you were and I thought—well I thought—I thought
Demetrius killed you. Say nothing of our marriage in
Theseus' palace with no memory whatsoever of a
ceremony. And Dad: like he's still in charge, with his
wall-eyed conviction, fear creasing his brow. "Something
there is that doesn't love it," that makes me want to take
an alias, lets fairies dew orbs, eggs Pyram and Thiz
on to risky behavior. Meanwhile I drink myself sober.
Get Philo over there to pour another triple sec.

The Beautiful Move

Here's what's left of the wall we had to build
out of shelves from the whatnot.
Soon as we finished, we bought cosmos
from the Portcullis Kiosk to sell by the carload.
We had to bail out the birds
who stole the beef and spit it in the harbor.
A smooth move, that bird trick.
Equally beautiful the way we got them off
like mountains built on slag
we sunk in dunes. We learned to calculate
profits using Pyle's equations.
After work we let our hair down.
But you: you came from the canon; you had
responsibility you couldn't back out on.
Like help's arch-android
we moved so as not to annoy you. We slept
in the dark. Watered flowers in the park
shaded your head from hazy sun.
We were the Angelus sung by the field ox
nested with the titmouse.
We helped it write a titmouse song.
And when the leopard came and we failed
to protect you we kept this commitment:
forced to choose between
ambivalence and stricture, we paid you half
by whole and told you what we
sold you wasn't whole and wasn't half.

Recycling *New Yorkers*

I almost let my subscription lapse
then nine eleven came
and even if the words had to be
drawn through pipes
too low to make out
and full enough of fog to sock us in
I needed the come one
come all of it.
I had to show my support.
On Monday I imagined
I was too wide awake
to stand on the sidelines
or go to the bathroom
out of earshot of the news.
Trains cut through the swamp
in summer sounding
close enough to
touch—and I thought
I'd purge my restless urges
biking down the side
of a Mexican pyramid.
At first I was scared and dizzy
but I liked how
the path held itself aloof from the hills
while at the same time
blending in with them
which must've distracted me
from the difficulty
because without the slightest effort
or clue as to how I was
staying on, I was staying on.

To Watch a Train

They show me their catwalk:
patches of shiny linoleum
and splintered planks with popped
nail heads and holes
I see through: someone
in the bathroom downstairs
looking up as we creak
above. I think what if
they were getting out of the tub.
One side of the catwalk
has a ten-foot drop to a sunken
den—and no railing.
My kids play with theirs.
I say "I hope you plan on adding
a railing." They say "Soon as we
get more wood." I nod
and they take me to a room that
looks out on a trainyard
three blocks away. Rust-colored
freight cars float between
distant sheds. All you see from
our windows are windows
in cars and windows
in houses. Shades go up
in the morning. Shades coming
down at night. But this rolling-stock
parade. This I'll have
another beer and dwell on.

No Different Than Crows

Birds are like weather: Once gone
it's hard to tell where they were.
One cardinal tripped the wire and so
it was recorded, though none of
this is verifiable. Like a physical
attentiveness clotted by veins,
this attempt to limber the neck,
this strain after the mouthful running
from the fountain. Crows' diet
leaves nothing to boast of—though
it keeps feathers well-oiled
and shiny. They might charcoal their
beaks or pick the webs off their
wings. Critics say they're clumsy:
they ought to peel back the onion.
What grace they manage they
abandon as soon as they come
to the table where they encounter
their betters' opposable thumbs
live from their mothers and
cold. Their very breath deprives
others of their livelihood. Crows
know this and prefer whirligigs,
canaries, Fourth of July white noise
whistling of the troops.

Dreaming Alone and with Others

Friends pulled one another away from the doors of girls
who didn't want to see them anymore.
They saved one another, they thought, from doing something rash.
And they might've been right:
They might've had a hard time taking no for an answer.
And the times they took each other's keys
when they knew they shouldn't drive
probably saved their lives.
Now they want to tell each other how to get better
deals on cell service and car repairs
and how much insurance to buy
—a whole raft of life-coach strategies and life lines
they should seriously grab.
Some of them like to feel their way in the dark.
Friends
continue looking out for them
despite their lack of appreciation. One turned down a job
another offered, saying the stars were all wrong.
He only said it
because he couldn't return the favor.
One put the chain on the door
and someone broke in with a hammer.
They left a note saying they should have a bigger TV,
smaller speakers for their sound system,
that their bracelets should be solid
gold, not plated.
They said they had nothing worth fencing.
That they should install dead-bolt locks and security
cams they could monitor with their phone.

Let's Talk

These droppings: they're yours,
aren't they? Well, let's let the attendant
finish peeling them off his knees.
Let's let the woodpecker
find the hootenanny with
three piebald pileateds standing
on one leg through 14 consecutive
renditions of "The Star-Spangled Banner."
Next thing you know
they're out fertilizing leaf mold.
Talk about your stiff salutes. But
who ever heard of singing pictures?
I know they're often signed.
A name or nativity scene can be sewn
into the label of all the hair-shirts
singled out for distribution,
but only the rare bird can knock out
a tune that visually cool.
Who wouldn't give it up for so much
butter in the beak? There's wood
to digest before we continue.
Never mind that you can't tell
who's fake and who's dealing true.
If you can't trust a picture
can you trust your intuition?

Gentry

Right here, right in the middle of what was once a thriving neighborhood and is now a half-abandoned stretch of city blocks—there's this restaurant—one of those franchised links in an up-and-coming chain—taking up the whole street-level of a relatively well-preserved brick storefront. There's a crowd of people at the tables—none of them looking like they come from around here. I'd say they're mostly expressive of privilege—though some look desperate enough—in a Thoreauvian kind of way. My father takes my hand. My grandmother says look, we're almost there.

Alecto

You knew I disliked their flapping so
you had your doves fold their wings.
It made me think of evening primrose
—for which I love you now with no
control. But it wasn't till you wrapped
summer's mist in gauze and cured
the cattle of their colds that I knew I'd
have to snub my sponsors, the makers
of PIZZAZZ where my position is
hard to gauge and I feel I'm getting
even, even as I feel I can't go on.
I told you how they accused me of
spitting in the indigo—nothing more
than muddled dregs and bitter resentment.
I only bring it up having had it out
with a prophet whose Voice Like
His Master the Rain set him on your
shining path. He said he knows you
better than I could ever hope to. He says
I should forget you, feed my kids
and fill my void on militating charity.
But I won't leave you in the company
of priests. I'd be less than loss of faith
would leave me. I dwell on you in
the arms of other women. I keep our
rapprochement: my inner circle small,
my hands off your sisters, applaud
your vagaries. You string me along.

Caliban in Jodhpurs

    Note: the knotted strand of her spine
approximates a raised dotted trestle.
    ...But she won't leave the water
    so I take to watching boys.
Small ones swimming, skimming stones, catching jellyfish and tadpoles.
Large ones on the court by the city pool. Their basketball skill
you don't often see on the screen.

You see it on the broad side of a barn though,
projected by abdominal contractions
originating in the chaff we fail to remove from our wheat.
A few years from now the roof will
collapse in a twenty inch snowfall,
killing three lambs, when it should have handled thirty.

I've taken many such holidays with the lights on,
and it's not likely this will be the last.
If anyone should see me looking too longingly I'll
shift the blame to the perimeter stare of Miranda.
Her name's supposed to be French, but it isn't
like she has
    a pearl on her tongue
    held in place by a stickpin. Like
sucking on a mint night and day.
    Which she does.
    Though her singing might be perfect

her tongue gives a certain inflection

—not unlike a lisp,
an overcompensation by way of articulate labials
—a lilting, careful spill of pearls and dimes.

She reminds me of the sandman.
Her voice soft grained, her back Braille,

her skin dripping, wet mouth poised
for blowing powder from her spoon.
    Will she

sing me to sleep with an antidote for longing,
or sop me with a chloroform raga?

Intellectual Property: Keep Out

There's a tunnel leading from the cellar
that looks straight
but it's so long you don't see the end.
With its low ceilings, cracked
floors, windowless and doorless walls,
it might tend
left or right or gently corkscrew out
of sight. What it does
is imperceptible. And the stairwell:
you can't tell up from down.
Thighs normally let you know you're
climbing and calves complain
descending, but here
muscles are clueless: It's two steps up
and two steps down
for mile after mile until you're thrust
out on a thousand-foot
perch where you float in the updraft
as if lifted off an O'Keeffe
desert like a kite in the shape of one
of her uterine skulls.
You wave your crimson tails while
blood drools from the snout
of a doe far below on a road far away.

I Feel a Little Drummy—If You Don't Mind My Saying

How fast it unraveled and how
to put it all behind is
beyond me: A past near a fountain
her son Tim stuck his feet in
and just like that
without taking time to clear
my throat I'm lighting
the wrong end of a cigarette
taking communion in the mouth
buying groceries at midnight.
I was in the kitchen
when her father fell—blood like
mud dripping from his lip.
She ran to him while her mother
posed for a Polaroid
standing on a stool
at the edge of the porch.
I haven't seen them in months
then the other day
I run into Tim. The kid he's
with says "Who's that?"
"He was" he says "my mom's"
and clears his throat.
I feel a twinge and burning
in my thigh, stick my hand in my
pocket and pull out
the still-lit crumpled end of a
cigarette. We lived together
almost a year. He could've said
I was a kind of stepdad.
He could've said I was his
mother's boyfriend.
He tells the kid I was her date.

Palm Frond in Candy Land

Good Friday on the hustings and here we go
pitching tents in the weeds around
our young-at-heart TV. And here's the guy
whose speech keeps us watching:
whose father had nothing but a mattress
from which to spout his jeremiads.
Now the son pinches loaves and fishes in our
streams and we thank him for the privilege:
We pledge financial support where
in the old days we'd have
ridden him out on a rail. I wouldn't mind
but my kids are in and out of his wagon.
And it's not so much the laying on of hands
as the cigarette burns and roadside pool.
It's an oppositional stance
I talk myself into—a trick I mince in winter
when crowds are thin and I'm sitting
on my hands. Words flow from the lip
like birdsong—like someone
has to hammer it into the soft blubbery anvils
of our pineal glands: "Forget the afterlife.
Drink and be merry. It's all
that's left when sex goes south. With luck
you don't linger. Friends: attractive
strangers, gifts like the sun giving warmth."

Pyongyang Arrival: Our Battlefield in Grisaille

It was learning he was alive—I'd seen and spoken to him
—known all along and only recently forgotten
that his death had been rumor, his funeral dream, the night
I'd taken his son for apparition, nightmare.

He was taller than I remembered and not so old
for all his ninety-five. There were chapters he'd written
in *The History of Spring and Unearthing of Its Future*
that chronicled his flight from an emissary that
the more I think about it, the more I think it brought death.
That the book brought him back

that the past was brief, the future unstable: if any got
out it would claim to be the end of all trifling, as if to say
we're desperate, as if we had neighbors to appease

pretending absorption in books, or actually being absorbed
falling into the trap of burying the living. That's
what I told the kids so I wouldn't have to explain standing
on the porch in the middle of the afternoon

taking the air after their grandfather's funeral.
The idea of mourning a man who hadn't actually died
was disturbing, though not quite as disturbing

as the words he spoke, saying he would never
ruin anyone's reputation in order to live a few more years.
This wiped the smiles off our faces. As if
we'd never comforted a child or acted out of loyalty.

He said the future was better unlived, the government
doomed to the failure predicted in *The History of
Spring and Unearthing of its Future* and there was nothing
in the way of redemption to expect in this world.

III. Forgeries

Brochure (I'm Open to Suggestion)

You might notice the knees no longer
fit
in the beekeeper weigh station.
Other changes are also evident:
Nine threads of
prohibited speech
localized in the vocalic buffer
cause mix-ups in most messages.
You hear the register ka-chink
from the breakfront
but you're never clear if it's money
going out or money coming in.
It's an ever-moving target.
It's how the holographic heads
know what to do while you wonder
if they're real.
You think you see them noodling
over directories.
How important it is to ask
whether gross national product
is worth
converting into pay dirt.
Do bells ring true on all your recordings?
You want to sew them on flags
and wave them
above the radar hoping that'll
reset the signal
and stimulate the jiggle
that ceased to cover the spread.

Rebuilding Soil

Who was there when the superintendent announced plans
to turn half the parking lot into a vegetable patch.
"Next year: corn. What we can't eat or sell we'll give
to the food bank. In winter we'll freeze up a skating rink
and drink mulled cider. I tell you after the losses
and layoffs these last few years—isn't it time?"
As more of us crowded his office to shake hands
and say thanks, his modesty got the better of him
and he tried to downplay the deal. "Real estate's a buyer's
market and we'd likely take a loss, so why not show
each other what we mean by corporate green."
His voice trailed off, the bell rang and we trickled
back to work, or stopped at various stations to grab coats
and lunch pails on the way to lining up to punch out.
At the old plant we'd fan out over several blocks
crossing railroad tracks and busy streets to find our rides
but this new jobsite in the suburbs came with surplus
parking and most of us liked the thought of rebuilding soil.
As to what they found when they plowed it up:
Seventeen plastic yogurt containers and the hairbrush
of a strawberry blond. There was a lithograph
of a Soviet-style tractor in the act of knocking down
a dacha, a shopping cart, a low wall of climbing ivy,
a list of dirty tricks from a dead president's gym bag.
Claim checks from a flight that never landed.
A model of a plane that never landed. A box of
ichneumon wasps, a fairy tale in a bottle, an anonymous
symphony—the woodwinds fresh, the skeleton of a horse
—the part between the abdomen and thorax, a can
of moustache wax and a cameo brooch. They found
papers in Walt Whitman's handwriting, descriptions
of Patterson, Seneca Falls, Schenectady and The Palisades.
They dug up the memoirs of retirees. Some
proud of the strength they found to do their jobs
and raise their families. Others spoke of the love they felt
for various work husbands and work wives.

Hey, You Like Fishing

Something gives a low whistle
in the dark and soon whole
families buy guns
and join cults. They want milk
drawn from what they call
the one true source.
Feral dogs haunt the bridges.
Birds wend their way
through air vents and roost
in warehouse rafters.
Their song, two soft clipped
tweets, the workers
find unnatural. They say
trapped birds hurt
morale and should be
shown out or shot. The boss
says no. The birds are
free to come and go through
corrugated runnels where
ceiling meets wall.
The union rep says free
don't sing like frightened
mice. They call their
mates and pine for woods
where cones fall prey to fire.

Julio and the Spoiler

Your friend across the street is doing your wife. You say it's no good. She shouldn't have to run up and down the stairs like that. You tell him to make her crawl out a window on a ladder connecting your second-story bedrooms. At first it doesn't reach so you lash a board between ladder and bed post—and tell him to make her try it.

Maybe she tries leaving you instead and the train breaks down in a town known for street gangs and oath keepers. She stays with the passengers, with their wine and bits of cheese.

Maybe it's a card game you start while she's gone. You wait till it's over to tell her you looked in on her one-year-old: dead as a deer in the breakdown lane.

You're saying she killed her kid. If you testify, and she's condemned, she'll welcome lethal injection—anything to get away from you. But the way they spread the arms and tilt the gurney—so it looks like crucifixion? Maybe there'd be a stay. Maybe she'd be innocent, Cortazar. Maybe it was you.

Out Damn Spot: Drive-Thru Bikini-Wax Car Wash

At a time when Al was confined to organizing swap meets
—a sure bet he wouldn't venture near the stairs—
Darlene was macraméing his image
on a pillow sham.
She had him on his knees in a John Singer Sergeant pose,
the stars standing out so boldly on his sweatband
you'd have thought he harbored death rays.
He took one look, went out for a drink, and that was the last
we saw of him. His customers asked us
to drop-ship gondolas using next-day air and only charge
them for general delivery. We gave them
a stopwatch and a back pat.
Darlene took his accounts but we crossed paths along those
dotted lines. I worked
for the west branch, she worked on the Nile.
Neither of us saw or spoke to one another. Never saw
a picture or appeared in a film. I seldom appeared in person.
And it's not a question of, "Thirty years ago
these roads were bridle paths through
undivided landscape." You think you know a name
—a flash of recognition and the path is such a distant speck.
You eat and sleep in the place
you were born or do like Darlene whose kids don't
know it yet, but she's leaving, and she won't come back.

Marriage

To estimate the age of a cypress
check its afternoon pallor, then lift
its hood and add up its rings.
    If they don't slant leave them.
If they do, note it in the log.
With luck we never have to read it.
    That's what they told us
in school anyway. My handwriting
was shaky then and it was
still shaky when I spoke of cypress
in the kitchen window. Life
    improved somehow but my
penmanship didn't and we
    started throwing parties.
We've been planning this one
for months and the sun is going to
    set right as we're about
to cut the cake. And kids are always
on the list of guests who grunt
when they ought to howl.
    It's how they keep themselves
awake. What they say I have
no ear for. There are no words for
—though they show what
melted where the door was.

Stop—Hey, What's That Sound

I'd record what's on my mind and load it onto drones. I'd have a fleet of a hundred the size of dragonflies —with powerful speakers. I'd send them out to spread the gospel. People would be sick of them and shoot them down, but I wouldn't care: drones would be so cheap I could buy a thousand with money left over from paying the rent. The first message would be: "What's that sound? Did you hear that? What are you deaf? No. Speak up. Did you say something?" Then I'd upload ghost sounds that people would hear in the middle of the night. I'd add projectors to throw scary images on their walls—transmitters to take over their phones and TVs. I'd cause so much chaos and confusion they'd want to get me under control. It might not be easy.

Adam and Eve on a Sugarloaf

The apple was only Chapter One in our book
of hard troubles. In moonlit parks
in squares of faded capitals
we played at running rallies, hosting
garden-variety Rilke retreats full of
hand-me-down torch songs, crepe myrtle
and muscadine, the joy of having
taught our kid to hold hands crossing
Palisades in traffic. Now he's thirty
and our pretentiousness irks him
who once wanted nothing more than
to watch Rumpelstiltskin spin hot
licks across our twin tattoos.
The neighbors would bring their dogs
and together we'd ravel the silken
thread of friendship out in that
pride-of-place place. Which brings us
Chapter Two: Near the edge of an east-facing
cliff, the sunset behind us casts
half shadows at our feet. I say
our upper halves are on the mountain
across the valley. You say they
dissolve in the mist before they even
come close to reaching that distant
slope. And it's true. With all the graders
and spreaders backing up and
paving roads we'd rather were left
unimproved, we can only hope
our shadows dissolve us slowly
and drown our memories in dreams.

Between Lennon's Death and the Day Before Xmas

I pour pennies from a jar and stack them.
I roll them up in paper rolls and weigh
my pockets down with them.
I buy milk and feel foolish paying with pennies
but there aren't many ways to get rid of them.
If I take them to the bank they want to
verify my account: They don't like pennies
and they don't like handing out empty rolls.
Kids only like throwing them at each other.
So I spend them—four at a time
when a price ends in a nine. I put them
in the collection box for Ronald McDonald House.
I go a few cents over the dollar
at the gas pump and shed a few that way.
It takes two years, but after watching
the level in my jar steadily drop, I finally
spend my last cent. The other day
I paid a dollar fifty for coffee and became
for the first time in years not only
penniless but wholly coin-free. I think about
what it might mean to be truly penniless
and realize that I'm far too self-absorbed.
Life will catch up with me. Today's
lunch cost $10.66. I said, "Battle of Hastings."
My son said, "What?" The cashier
knew and gave a penny to the cause.

We Broke Ranks with Silence

It was Xmas in July, time to come clean
and tell the client what happened to the ashtray.
It was the kind of assignment that makes
diehards wish they'd stayed home.
Funny how tables can turn on you like that.
—How oversized dishrags convince us
to use them as cleaning aides. It was a near
threat that sent Wilbur up a ladder that no
longer made noise. He climbed it till he ran
out of rungs. He'd been on edge like that
ever since he had to gag his mother
and drag her in for a third evaluation.
He had never taken up smoking. He was
eight when she gave him permission.
Whenever he encountered an ashtray
it was like a kick in the groin. It made him
want to collect sweat bees to take his mind
off the skinned knees and bosses, the hawks
and wingspan-to-die-for cormorants
whose four-square necks reminded him of
the old days. He shouldn't have had that
much autonomy. He's in recovery now,
working through his Crosby and Nash as if
shattered glass still mattered, as if any of us
could stay young and stay together.

One of the Monuments Leans North

There has to be an explanation:
erosion, tree roots, frost heaves:
something that tilted the monument
off its axis, so that it pointed
skyward, not directly overhead,
maybe in collusion with some
more-than-human intelligence
real or imagined, hiding in plain
sight somewhere on the continuum,
using the monument to mark
a landing zone or conduit.
And maybe it sits on the grave
of someone whose influence
none of us can fathom. Some
Dickinson or Stearns. Some Mabel
Loomis Todd or her well-hung
astronomer husband. Or Susan
Gilbert, who exhumed her parents
just to bury them in Amherst.
Maybe we could get the family's
permission to set it right
as representing the way a loved
one ought to be remembered:
a spirit standing tall. Or maybe
drag the monument off its
pedestal before the whole town
starts to deconstruct around us.

Nihil Obstat

How refreshing: catching me with
Sonia
then pouring drinks and lighting
my cigar.
You might think
it was you deceiving me the way
you beg forgiveness.
You could have knocked me over
with your smile and surreal
solicitude.
Was that supposed to confuse? Or
make me feel small?
Did you
know all along Sonia and I were
fucking and plan this cool discovery?
Tell me, I'm waiting on pins
and needles.
I'd cry, but I bet you'll beat me to it.
—Go ahead. Add your
voice
to the honking of
geese and the gasping of the dying.

There Doesn't Seem to Be a Way to Feel Better

While my father was still around
for me to wrap my arms around
I held myself back. I didn't
want to ruffle the feathers of his
breastbone or listen to his heart's
sweet murmur. The feeling
would've been wrong. I wouldn't
want him feeling smothered.
I wouldn't want my sons doing it
to me if it felt the least bit
insincere. As if kangaroo aphids
were propped in the corners
of our grimaces. I'd thrash out
with war plans. A father can only
stand so much. The same goes
for sons. Their last best hope
is the spirit of the walking stick.

Underbelly

We watched from a window—we might've
gone in—but didn't stick. His estate
was a plot between cottages. His pennant
dotted with waves. Someone else
ran it up the flagpole—someone drawing
strength from the inner workings of the wall.
He acted like bricks had ears. He'd be like
somewhere else until a minute later.
He'd file for special status if the world
stopped holding up its claim. The old
boss was bold but I didn't like his big disdain.
The time he almost died they made us
assemble his underwear. They offered to
teach us design. Then he returned
—saying dying was easy. Compared to
being sick. It's a stance, I guess. While
the rest of us live on conditions. One solid.
One out of form—each from different sides
of the same instability—the nouveau
—and the old whose weight returned to kill him.
Lucky the door that harbors the pinup
the deep-fried hair bun, three socks
and two legs in one wadded-up sleeve.

Pallet (Or the Urge to Put My Socks On Standing Up)

He should have stood that
coffin lid between
columns of heavy cases
instead of laying it across
three layers and piling
eight cases of beer on top.
It stuck out more
than a foot and the layers
above didn't line up with those below.
The boss said fix it.
The kid took too much
off one side and the coffin
lid and two cases of beer
fell on the boss's foot.
He grabbed the kid
and said he saw a pet snake
eat a pet frog once in his
great aunt's garage but if
he had his way this snake
of a kid would be a bump
in a frog toad's gullet.
The kid said, been there
done that, in the belly
of the beast, and if the boss
didn't back right off
he'd bust him in the gut
and stuff him in the trash.
And now he's flipping
blinis and now he's sorting
ties and color-coding
labels for table scraps.

Moving On with Original Energy

Hard to keep from swallowing
that
bit of chewed-up mouthguard when
the tongue wants it bad.
Even jaws join the coalition
of the salivating. The only thing
to do is spit it out. It's more
than fear of choking;
it's knowing it's the grinding
of the mouthguard that keeps molars
whole.
It says it might cure headache
but some wounded animal hides it
in the dune grass
near the melon rind flies and bees
feast on—where it lacks
the dull gleam beachcombers
look for and like
all soft droppings
it wears the faint smile of offal.
It slips the sieve and no one
sees who doesn't follow its changes.
If they gag, they're dragged
to the swamp and left
with Jeffrey Amherst pillowcases
covering their faces.

Political Diatribe (Tripe)

I want to thank those who march through hell so that I might
walk around unmolested. I want to thank those who lost loved ones
in wartime, families and friends who deal with the bright
lights of grief. You're more deserving than I. What have I done
with this blessing, this noble experiment bought with your
hard-fought gains and unbearable loss? I made mud pies, dust devils
and snow angels; I made sandcastles and grass violins, nothing
if not ephemeral, a bit like taking other people's thoughts
and arranging them in ways that maybe make a different kind
of sense than they did to begin with. Some are like feathers
or trance-inducing fetishes, others like bits of the outdoors
brought in. I sit by the window, watch for the news to come from
on high, down to the valley where I break it up into digestible
fragments to make it easy for busy minds to swallow—I'm
like the *Popular Mechanics* of psychic awareness. I look at things
I think are pretty longer than anyone else I know. I look at
what you've done to get me where I am and judge some of it
to be not so pretty if you don't mind my saying. And you have
a right to mind. But I say it. I look for projects worthy of your sacrifice,
ones beyond sandcastles and mud pies. I'm still searching.

IV. Ingredients

T Is the Letter of the Day

It's like your face fits you to a T
as if your moods showed
in the lines around your eyes
and the creases of your mouth.
But what if the name that
went with your face showed
on a list of nonessential personnel?
Would you hop in the pocket
on the list's last page and hope
the purge people don't
think to look there? No list
can pocket itself but you can
hide in a pocket along with
the list and a list of pockets
can fit in any pocket big
enough to hold it. You could
take the list and slap it
on a soup can—or kick
yourself for not crossing
your name off before
the label nailed you on the lip
and the wrist broke in a
crooked-fingered handshake.
But they were never out to
get you that way—just
purge you off the payroll.
You still have something
to live on. Ivy on your
walls and hair. You tie it
in beard strings as if tomatoes
grew where nouns could
take the place of asterisks.
Debt relief permeates your
wherewithal. Big winds
rattle bars on all your cages.

Pass the Oblivion, Thank You

You make a liar out of me.
Call me Punchinello.
Say I've a load of deadwood
that won't hold up.
You'd play it by ear if it
meant a rosier forecast.
I offer to pay with a crumbly
chunk of cornbread,
the lurch inviting me
to leave you in it—I feel it
build like a spike
of jewelweed or purple
narcissus, straight but
impermanent like bad
trout spoiling what should
outlast a bus terminal
ceiling fan. I breathe
on a mirror while you sleep
and eat where plumbing
used to be an open
sewer. Two glasses
of cabernet: one you spill
on your Neo-con guest,
the other on the chair
where the kids used to
sit. They tout a pill
that counteracts what
age does to desire.
I take each mention
as a dig. They have pills
so you don't feel digs
and other pills so
you don't feel desire
—so you don't feel
the needle going in.
I want to feel it though.
I want to be aware.

Vacuity

Photographic memory. Know anyone who has one? I'd love to have one. I'd love to remember what was going on in certain dreamlike situations, like where the bridge was on the res, and what Kelly was doing there with her Bengal cats—up to then they'd been indoor cats, but they certainly seemed to be enjoying themselves, riding on one another's backs, frolicking in sun and shade, not straying, not losing sight of us and making us look for them. I wondered if it'd be that easy getting them back in the house. It occurred to me with a bit of a shock that I should get out of there and get to work, which I did eventually. Everyone was glad to see me, but I'd been gone so long I didn't have much of a job left. I had a workstation: the shell of a computer—with no screen. I couldn't do very much without a screen. It would've been great if my absence was work-related because I almost remembered being on some work-related mission and might've spun out an acceptable excuse that might've left me feeling secure in my position, though it would've been embarrassing, given that I had no supporting details about this hypothetical mission, and I got the feeling, listening to one of the assistant managers upbraid an underling in one of the cubicles—as if I needed reminding: I had no desire to work here anymore.

Inside Out

Nearly finished renovations: three
walls pale eggshell, the fourth
the same but richer, bolder.
The trim and baseboard something
in between and complementary
like the wrists and ankles
of a well-accessorized mannequin.
The furniture—better than new
though it's been here the whole time.
Floors stripped, polished and buffed
are softer and more comfortable
than the carpets that covered them.
We finish taking the tour
then look out the window at the street
more torn up and dilapidated than
ever. It seems we'll never
make the highway. Somehow we
do though. Leave the old apartment
and even if it did look fine we
won't miss it. Even if the ride is long
and the kids loud. Even if it rains.
We try to read but the kids
are loud. Then the rain stops and
the setting sun appears. We want
a picture of the skyline seen in
passing where a jade green mosque
glows. It's gone before we can
open a camera. The driver turns
to backtrack but it's too late.
The sun is gone and so is the glow.
Some of us want to go see the interior.
Some of us want to move on.

Home Sweet Homicide

It was such a long way to hang out the window
to hug our wives and daughters
we almost didn't take the time.
We had the feeling we could whip the skin
off a snake
with a snap of the wrist
and that feeling meant more to us than sons
and daughters and wives.
Actually, we could twist the snake's head
to loosen the flesh
and pull the marbled meat off its thick fat skin
like it was nothing
—though
we never got the chance to eat it.
It always rose like the slain cattle of Helios
and we had to
get a ladder to pull it down.
I can't tell you what a fool's errand that was.

See Emily Alone

Alone in her room, thinking about the garden
—the work her mother and sister put into it
day in day out month after month for decades:
their intimate knowledge of flora and fauna
what to eat, what to avoid. She does her part
but not much lately, and neighbors want to
know what she's up to. The following is typical
of responses she gives well-meaning inquiries:
"You know, there's a recipe I've been
reconstructing—the list of ingredients burned
on the stove, and Mrs. Goff whom I got it from
has since died—The cake was delicious;
it opened you to transports. Now my only hope
is to sit with an open mind in the same place
where I first read it. So far I've managed to
retrieve a bit. I believe by the end of the century
while I may not be so much in evidence my
cake will and I think you will say it was well
worth the wait." Her notes include drawings
and references to near-forgotten founder crops,
entries for poultices made from the bark of
spreading yew. One from the rind of quince
refers to an entry for mole flies: "bites cause
wasting fever if left untreated after 10 days."

Twenty-oh-Two: Between the Provocation and Revenge

A limpet bit me, my teeth hurt and
I've got a sore throat. I ought to
put the kids to bed and call it a night
but a singer named Bjork is
hopping around on Local Access 12.
Her voice is haunting, her dance
has me watching, her draped white
sleeves basted to the bodice of her
dress as if they're bats' wings.
She wiggles her fingers and I wiggle
back. She wants me to believe she
can entertain in ways having little
to do with sex. As if she's an angel.
Why not, if it's all in my head?
I notice the camera keeps leaving her
to hover over the hand that works
the controls. The moon spills across
the stage. It knows the show was recorded
on what might've been a moonless
night—but the camera won't stay
on her and here's a moon that will.
Suddenly, she lets out a clear high
note and one by one all the kitchens
in Connecticut light up like it's
suppertime in winter. Now the neighbors
want in: Every city and town and
every school of fish from Paris
to La Jolla. And the camera shifts.

Morning Song for Robert J.

When he lost his ocarina he didn't spend much time looking.
Instead he strapped a tape recorder over his shoulder
—it made him feel like he wasn't playing with a full deck
but he did it anyway. He stayed out from four
in the morning every day until dawn. Until the eighth
of May there was nothing but wind, light traffic, the slap
of his boots in the dark and his breathing.
And then he heard it. With the first glimmer of dawn the woods
came alive. He captured a recording. Some of it sounded
like an ocarina, but there was more. A symphony in trees.
A universe in branches. Some near some far
and everything between. Whistle chat warble low squeaky
dove-moan catcall soft reedy peep and piping calling
responding cheering jeering shrieking jabber honk and fluting
—all of it influencing the music he wrote and performed
on piano and bassoon, some scored for orchestra
until he and his wife started a family, needed more reliable
income and he began programming classical music
for Public Radio's Boston affiliate in the last days of the Nixon era.
Soon stations were syndicating his show
coast to coast beginning each morning with the chorus
at dawn—something to tickle the high end of your
speakers while the deep patient cadence of his voice
worked the woofers. Somewhere between 8 and 9 he'd read
news taking deep breaths in the middles of
sentences never betraying what he thought of the war.
By eighty-eight things had run their course.
One station after another cut him down to an hour or went
wholly over to *Morning Edition.* He retired and died
and nobody hears the dawn chorus unless they rise
at 5 a.m. in May or play an old copy of *Close to the Edge.*

Funding Subversives in a Dry Cold Clime

By August 10th the birds had seen a ghost and fallen silent.
Someone said they sometimes follow children
and we said who, the ghosts or the birds and they said
Emily. Or Dorothy. Not Evangeline, though she'd have
given up the ghost long before she listened to her husband.
He said you've no idea what it's like to solve a puzzle
until you dangle from the roofline in the middle of
washing windows. He said you have to write
a hundred-page memo every month to keep the meaning
of existence from slipping through the harness. Otherwise
things could be worse: our eyes could open one
spring morning to find ourselves bound for some foreign
land instead of waking to windows jammed shut
while children sing and birds pluck the worms in clover.

Refresher Training Vid

You won't find a faster, more efficient Self-Inducing
Terra-Former anywhere from here to Mars.
So why is Jupiter dropping us for Gentex Moto-Gucci
Hoff-whatever? It's not a question of rigged bids
or bug-ridden code and it's not as if we miss deadlines.
No one's undercutting price points and it's not about
quality. So what went wrong? I'll tell you what:
One of our call center operators referred to their rep
as Ron instead of Don. Camel Springs squatters
and Death Valley transplants will be having us for
breakfast before we ever do that again. So here's the plan:
We train. We practice. As in the following example:
Pretend I'm Client X on his thirty-fucketh birthday:
chocolate stucco on his shaved cherubic cheeks.
He shits and his mother loves it; peace and prosperity
in the good-and-lofty pin work of his diaper,
longevity in the weave of his tie. We see by the way
he tips his hand: his flush is no way royal: no
king, no ace, no jack-loving queen he can lean on.
He raises rabbits—and that's our in. We build a hutch
and a hot tub in his artificial garden. We buy
him lunch and mix him up a three-martini moon.

I Went to a Small Island

in the Aegean where flightless birds
navigate rivers and streams
like penguins but with three times
the number of nerve endings
and capillaries in their fins.
They communicate while swimming:
a cross between signing and telepathy.
You never hear them coming.
They're just there putting
thoughts in your head. I heard
they could help break negative habits.
Help you quit blaming yourself
for big and little flaws.
I heard people quit smoking
after swimming with a bird that flapped
its fins at a rate that mirrored
the echo of the human heartbeat.
I spent a month hoping
they'd fill me with endless cheer.

Ewer

Quite the find, that cross between garden supply
and butterfly bodega. Giant tiger-lily monarchs parking
on your shoulder while tiny lace-wing moth types
nestled in your hair. The whole thing made us hungry
but the place was crawling with pizza eaters. Then
I realized it was the same time last week when we
couldn't get a table and—our kids—where were they?
I asked the owner if he had any idea. He was standing
near a shelf full of nasal sprays and condiments
holding a glass of water in his loosely bandaged hand
and I couldn't help wondering whether there'd be
room near the lemons. I was thinking stoneware jug
in pink terracotta with indigo veins—not the stainless
steel buckets you see in hospitals—and the pewter
spittoons of bars—just a simple, modest classic as a
way to say thanks. But the waitress was a student
I once failed for plagiarizing. She had a look like
she was only two thoughts from coming after us with
daggers. I wanted to say this was it for jobs if she
didn't drop the attitude, but her boss might take it
as an insult. Then he might not tell us where our kids
were. So I let it go, and in letting it go it slipped
and fell out on the floor—and I knew right then our
outing was in trouble—we'd dropped the kids in line
for the Ferris wheel—it must have been hours ago.
We fairly flew the ten blocks but we found them.
The power had failed soon after they climbed aboard
and they'd been in tears near the top ever since.

Plateau

If you should miss the cairn
you might spot the goat
nibbling sage or hear what
the wind does to the sound
of his cowbell.
You might find the blind
I watch eagles from.
I might be there, where it
hardly ever rains. When
it does, I catch it in buckets.
Just don't mistake me
for the girl who ran from
drought to drowning. Or
confuse my shadow with
the lodgepole pine. I'm not
that tall. I stand on stumps
to see the big picture
to wait for kestrels to break
from the clouds, their cries
remodel the mountain,
a sound that drowns
in the updraft even as
it rumbles up through stone.

I Swam into You by Accident

The Blue Line trail is all cool indirection:
it skirts beaten paths and levees,
leads through bogs that sink footprints
and erase the traces of passage,
begrudging return, as who
wouldn't want to stay where broken bottles
settle scores on the rocky shore
of a lake supposed to be haunted?
A busted pump house juts from an outcrop.
Faded graffiti hints at petroglyphs
of spiral jetties in a smooth
windward wall. Looking vaguely
pre-Navajo: In one breath a starry encounter
a nest of threads at antennae-like
angles and the careless
could be in for a swim. Maybe find
an underwater cave and come out in Ohio.
Maybe get tangled up in
mangrove roots. Or stay on the path,
vary the length of a measure, leap
through hollows and spin a new cocoon.

Pueblo

1. Building

Our city: warm on the outside, cool as kicks
within. It tricks us out of the desert and into
messing with our outsized selves. It records
conversations and reduces our memories to crystals
so that news of our impending extinction hangs
like static in afternoon sun. And though
we don't lack strength of numbers and we barely
remember the tune, when we see ourselves set
in grayscale lines and grainy staves, the fields,
woods and nesting grounds silent, only the colors
intact, the grays and inky greens, the sky-blue
backdrops shrunk into cubes, they shroud us
in silence. They set us in rows like dominoes,
a seeding of clouds, a quick rubbing of hearts.

2. Evening

Tonight we pray, each to our separate familiar:
We ask for nothing beyond their tacit
approval, though we haven't needed approval
since taking our problems into our small but
capable hands. We think of gods as insects.
We feel them couple, uncouple. We feel they're
part of a game, a brim field of hosts that listens
for anthrax vaccination tracks that rattle
our cages and force us up through hazes of
smoke rings and post-hypnotic cues full of cupcake
and ash where teeth chatter in cadence
and hearts leap to the castanets of Maya.

3. Morning

Dawn's insomniacs argue over kisses that kill
and pills that keep us alive: twin telescopes
that watch from a cross-canyon window, shot
through with light poured from a wound and falling
through skies of county-fair diamonds, still
blond and blue-green, still brief as a golden age.

4. Remembering

Sons call stepfathers, blisters forming in their
mouths. They call us Pueblo. They call us
perfect parents. They cling to illusions and revise
family history. They won't forget faces
—not the ones they found and not the ones
lost in dime-store delinquent rapture
watching stars increase their
number as the number of nights spent nosing
the classifieds, falling on used slightly
soiled, still viable leases on hogans whose
doorjambs sough with ice and the exhalations
of hyrax, asking if stories, asking if
homes bare heads to Orion, looking down
to an unseen gulf, across the neighboring mesa,
the anthill we dream, solid rock
home of light, home alone, or in a crowd.

Acknowledgments

The writer gratefully acknowledges the following journals and reviews:

2River View: "No Different Than Crows"
88: "Caliban in Jodhpurs"
Abridged: "I Feel a Little Drummy—If You Don't Mind My Saying"
Alternative Reel: "Alecto"
Anti-Heroin Chic: "It Starts"
Appalachian Review: "I Swam into You by Accident"
Barnwood: "Silver Queen Corn"
Citizens for Decent Literature: "Political Diatribe (Tripe)"
Lyre Lyre: "The Beautiful Move"
Meat for Tea: "Twenty-oh-Two: Between the Provocation and Revenge," "See Emily Alone"
Naugatuck River Review: "Morning Song for Robert J."
Poetry Pacific: "There Doesn't Seem to Be a Way to Feel Better"
Prick of the Spindle: "Rust"
Silkworm: "Big Blind Little Blind," "Home Sweet Homicide"
The Bicycle Review: "Let's Talk"
The GW Review: "Large Building in Which to Lay Aside Your Shame"
The Pedestal: "Ewer"
The Straddler: "Moving On with Original Energy"
The Valley Advocate: "One of the Monuments Leans North"
Tidal Basin Review: "Land of Little Sticks Again"
Tongue Magazine tonguemag.co.uk: "Hey Herm, look at Snout: dressed like a wall!" "This Is My Letter to the World"

"I Went to a Small Island" first appeared in the anthology *Poeming Pigeons* (The Poetry Box, 2015).

About FutureCycle Press

FutureCycle Press is dedicated to publishing lasting English-language poetry in both print-on-demand and Kindle formats. Founded in 2007 by long-time independent editor/publishers and partners Diane Kistner and Robert S. King, the press was incorporated as a nonprofit in 2012. A number of our editors are distinguished poets and writers in their own right, and we have been actively involved in the small press movement going back to the early seventies.

Each year, we award the FutureCycle Poetry Book Prize and honorarium for the best original full-length volume of poetry we published that year. Introduced in 2013, proceeds from our Good Works projects are donated to charity. Our Selected Poems series highlights contemporary poets with a substantial body of work to their credit; with this series we strive to resurrect work that has had limited distribution and is now out of print.

We are dedicated to giving all of the authors we publish the care their work deserves, offering a catalog of the most diverse and distinguished work possible, and paying forward any earnings to fund more great books. All of our books are kept "alive" and available unless and until an author requests a title be taken out of print.

We've learned a few things about independent publishing over the years. We've also evolved a unique and resilient publishing model that allows us to focus mainly on vetting and preserving for posterity poetry collections of exceptional quality without becoming overwhelmed with bookkeeping and mailing, fundraising activities, or taxing editorial and production "bubbles." To find out more about what we are doing, come see us at futurecycle.org.

The FutureCycle Poetry Book Prize

All original, full-length poetry books published by FutureCycle Press in a given calendar year are considered for the annual FutureCycle Poetry Book Prize. This allows us to consider each submission on its own merits, outside of the context of a traditional contest. Too, the judges see the finished book, which will have benefitted from the beautiful book design and strong editorial gloss we are famous for.

The book ranked the best in judging is announced as the prize-winner in January of the subsequent year. There is no fixed monetary award; instead, the winning poet receives an honorarium of 20% of the total net royalties from all poetry books and chapbooks the press sold online in the year the winning book was published. The winner is also accorded the honor of being on the panel of judges for the next year's competition; all judges receive copies of the contending books to keep for their personal library.

www.ingramcontent.com/pod-product-compliance
Lightning Source LLC
LaVergne TN
LVHW020049110826
845155LV00029B/698

9781952593376